81 AUSTERITIES

SAM RIVIERE

81 Austerities

faber and faber

First published in 2012
by Faber and Faber Ltd
Bloomsbury House
74–77 Great Russell Street
London WC1B 3DA

Typeset by Faber and Faber Ltd
Printed in England by T. J. International Ltd, Padstow, Cornwall

A CIP record for this book
is available from the British Library

ISBN 978–0–571–28903–5

FSC
www.fsc.org
MIX
Paper from
responsible sources
FSC® C101712

2 4 6 8 10 9 7 5 3 1

Contents

Acknowledgements

I am grateful to the editors of the following online and print publications where some of these poems have previously appeared: *Adventures in Form*, *Ambit*, *Clinic Presents*, *Days of Roses*, *Etcetera*, *Eyewear*, *Infinite Editions*, *Internet Poetry*, *Magma*, *New Statesman*, *NewWriting.net*, *Poetry London*, *Poetry Review*, *Silkworms Ink*, *Unsure if I will allow my beard to grow for much longer*, *Unswept.* and *White Review*.

Thank you to everyone who followed this project in its original form online. Thanks especially to Sophie Collins, George Szirtes, Jack Underwood, Emily Berry, Edmund Gillingwater, Rachael Allen, Sam Buchan-Watts, Sylvia Whitman and Shakespeare & Co., Nathan Hamilton, Harry Burke, Matthew Gregory, Tim Cockburn, Steven Fowler, Jeremy Noel-Tod, Matthew Hollis.

Thank you to my brother, sister, mother and father.

Austerity was named the word of the year
by Merriam-Webster in 2010.

GIRLFRIEND HEAVEN

Crisis Poem

In 3 years I have been awarded
£48,000 by various funding bodies
councils and publishing houses
for my contributions to the art
and I would like to acknowledge
the initiatives put in place
by the government and the rigorous
assessment criteria under which
my work has thrived since 2008
I have written 20 or 21 poems
developed a taste for sushi
decent wine bought my acquaintances
many beers many of whom have
never worked a day in their lives
how would you like to touch my palm
and divine how long my working
week has been mostly I watch films
and stare and try to decide what
to wear speaking as a poet I would
rather blow my brains out than run
out of credit as the biographer
of the famously unresolved
50s poet-suicide has commented
capital is the index of meaning
anything is better than stealing
from the Co-op with a clotted heart
without it you don't survive

My Real Name Is

Saori Hara born 1st January 1988 Adult Video idol
face of anti-STD campaigns & star of Tokyo 20xx
who is to appear in the world's first 3D adult movie
whose memoir *My Real Name is Mai Kato: Why I
Became an AV Girl* was published December 2009
and details what 'goes on inside an AV Girl's head
during filming' and contains the lines 'The actor
opened his hand in front of me. It seemed really wet,
filled with sweat . . . But then I realised the wetness
was from me, from down there. At that moment,
it was spurting out of me. I felt messy, ashamed
& sad. A lot of feelings were in my heart & mind,
combating one another, & just like that it was over.'

As Himself

She is not an especially good judge of character
as evidenced by her choice of confidant
your disputably virtued 'speaker'

[No Subject]

can we think about getting the internet
reconnected & also a terrestrial TV aerial
going to cafés to email is so depressing
tell me why did we let the internet
unmoor its radiant cloud from
above our home when choosing what
to watch on demand is too stressful
obviously I am not going to 'choose'
to watch *How I Met Your Mother*
if it's on I don't have that problem

Sad Dads of the Girlfriends

I wonder did you think beyond this point
of whole days to dream of what
like a bright key dropped straight
to the bottom of a well your spectacles
warping programmes in the sitting room
you finally use where evenings tighten
to a funnel the TV's zap-line equals sleep
and later to wake for an hour thinking clearly
your silences like streetlights coming on
your stories slowly going nowhere past them
O daughters come away from the windows
lie down here and tell me what you've spent.

Clones

As she climbs onto the mattress to lay out
with Anselmo, the food was spiffy
and the drilled back sextoy is great
but satisfying 1 appetite stimulates another.
So guys love latina virgins in swimsuit.
And what a collection of buttholes.
The perverts at duke dollars are exploiting women
at the lowest level of scum you can imagine
for your entertainment dollar, humiliation
is on flash here. You got ass, you got
potatoes, you got rapier suckin,
coral pummelling and the whole nine.

Cuts

I can see that things have gotten pretty bad
our way of life threatened by financiers
assortments of phoneys and opportunists
and very soon the things we cherish most
will likely be taken from us the wine
from our cellars our silk gowns and opium
but tell me what do you expect Chung Ling Soo
much ridiculed conjurer of the court and last
of the dynasty of brooms to do about it?

The Sweet New Style

she looks out of her
photos let's call her emma
with a mute appeal that might
mean something like 'whenever
you want just say I'm ready to be taken
away from all this' she is so shy
her eyes follow your eyes
over the girlish slopes and crests
hidden by her baggy cardigan jennifer
I mean emma let me assure you
your shyness has never been
so completely justified

And There the Resemblance Ends

what can I suggest we do instead
I'm not saying anyone should stop
give up and find a job every day
I lug my ache around the cemetery
it seems I learnt this slump I had
to not think it being born not guilty
and preferring certain polluted fruits
you're not supposed to like it
but it could make you feel 'quaint'
the alternative is beyond words
bad though no-one will force you
to wear a theft square on your face
if I sense you're struggling that's
because it doesn't rhyme with you
in any way today I didn't look
in anyone's eyes so *what* debts
I didn't see you there we haven't
met is it unbearable to read
the names on graves as titles
it's all material the monumental
there's no telling and well if you
want what's stopping you nothing

GRAVEBERRIES

Crumbs

The way she perches on the red velveteen cushions
appearing to feel that to lean back or look relaxed
would be to display an unwholesome fondness
for luxury & therefore a noticeable weakness

The Pinch

It never ceases to astonish or offend me
seeing the couples circulate the otherwise
dead town centre like leaves in a big ashtray
in a sort of drugged calm they're dreamy I guess
linked limply they don't see where the other looks
& the sun doesn't bother to lift its head from the table
but is leaking torpid 'honeyed' light from behind clouds
imagine it living for years and years with the same person

Premises Premises

went to see Factory Floor at the George
sort of chronically depleted noisecore
doom drones and metronomes 'jittery
post-punk agitators' do you remember
their rehearsal space with all the lists
the gaffer and duct tape on everything
what the sound guys call 'drum cancer'

The Mysterious Lives of the Stars

I want something what is it
those little boobies from 1964
in the Willy Ronis exhibition
in something like somebody's
new raspberry sweater I don't
wear sunglasses though
I like opacity I like that you
can't see my expression as
I'm sitting writing this
in my favourite T shirt the one
with the retro pin-up girl
listening to a black telephone on it
& with yellow armpits like Rimbaud
bless the powers that have taken
our grievances away from us

Gothic Poem

wider than a library
& strewn with flyleaves
torn from 2nd-hand novels
a grave lays in a plot of sun like
an abandoned picnic & somewhere
nearby a green bonfire in the background
a maroon lawnmower rides onto the pavement

You There in the Shadows

come out where I can see you
through the dense mist of my cataracts
perhaps you bring me news of my daughter
who was married and shipped two moons ago
no perhaps then you have come bearing gifts a case
of the local grape of which in my later years I have become
inordinately fond no I can see from your expression I'm mistaken
ah you have brought the reply from the queen of Spain a resounding yes

The Handsoap Cares

it's stopping snowing as bedhead comes on my headphones
on the top deck I'll have to walk home in the cold again
just like last time I should've brought my bobble hat
but feel bad seeing jenny wearing the hat emma
knitted me so   it's started snowing again

Dream Poem

I know what you're thinking
it's dull unless they're sex dreams
dreams about violent murders
mine are pretty banal
I dreamed I wrote a poem
beginning 'Hi!' and ending 'See You Later!'
the middle part was amazing
that's the part I don't remember
I was sitting on a platform high above the jungle
this all feels really familiar
probably from something I've seen on TV
I was dressed up as a witch doctor
and used this stick of judgement
taking back the names of creatures
restoring them to myth I was doing wisely with it
in my dream the poem didn't have
this assonance that's creeping in
after I'd taken back everything
I kept hold of my stick using it
to designate the categories that really matter
while adding bones and wings to my hat
sitting up here out of danger
I hate this / I like that

Adversity in the Arts

personally i can't remember   hearing of a time there was so much
well-written work being produced   all of it extremely well-written
S's first novel is excellent   H's new collection is also excellent
i'm told how nice it is to see that I   T and E finally have their
books out i'm sure they'll receive   excellent reviews in the broadsheets
it's no exaggeration to say that   there are not enough minutes
in the day to give each the attention   they undoubtedly deserve

SPOOKY DUST

Confessional Poem

I was watching TV
    with the window open
        it was a warm night
            when the phone rang
        it was light where you
    were calling from the scene
of a serious car accident
    in fact you were dying
        of all the friends you
            could have rung
        you'd chosen me to find
    a meaning of some kind
to end your life or rhyme

Closer

this is the part where
he faces an ornate mirror
prods his varnished complexion
seems heroic
and demonstrates genre savvy
by changing his accent
an ambiguous clone ending
in the right hands creates
a powerful sense of an indifferent universe
in the wrong hands creates
pretentious crap

Sensors are Tingling

Old books smell like turning fruit
I can't read any more John Wieners
before my baseball comes unstitched
and the cotton stuffing fluffs out
a bit like old peach or soft nectarine
before my boiled beetroot leaks its juice
staining the blue shirt from Paris
it took me ages to work out where
in my room it was coming from
before the android looks at the
gaping hole caved in his chest
the android that thinks he's a man

'94

what an amazing year
so many great albums
look it up for yourself
I'd get nostalgic but
unfortunately no one
around here could care
too much about the 90s
meanwhile you were
what 6 how does that
make you feel it's really
hard to tell now you are
linked to ≈10000 images
it's funny in my fantasies
I'm the one who dies
you stay here looking as
always excellent in black

New Crew

mm isn't it funny in films
when they say 'hang on
this isn't a movie' or else
'c'mon man it's the *1970s*'
that little nod beyond the screen
it ruins everything for me
the actor is a LIAR with
a liar's face a liar's insistence
keeping his story straight
dude it's better to come clean
this is a movie it is 4 reel

No Touching

I would like to ruin your life
let it not be said I lack the necessary
imagination to be jealous
I would ask you to tell no one about us
and if you tell no one about us
I'll fight hard to hide my disappointment
I would like you to renounce your past
as quite a big mistake
it will mean something although I
will never completely forgive you
I think you represent
the possibility in my life of renewal
I would like people to say
'she came back a different person'
we will appear at the weddings
of people we don't care about
our faces radiant from fucking

Year of the Rabbit

there is no purer form of advertising
than writing a poem
that's what the monk told me
if I were a conceptual artist
I would make high-budget trailers
of john updike novels but no actual movie
the scene where angstrom drives towards
the end of his life down a street in the suburbs
lined with a type of tree he's never bothered
to identify and laden with white blossoms
reflecting slickly in the windscreen
I would fade in the music
as the old song was fading out
keeping the backing vocals at the same distance
kind of balancing the silence
the word RABBIT appears in 10-foot trebuchet

Loosely Spiritual American Poetry

vs. tensely materialistic british poetry
vs. tireless love poetry of eager administrators
vs. tiring political poetry of benefit fraudsters
vs. improvised poetry of nomadic herdsmen
vs. impoverished poetry of the fully funded
vs. lavish poetry of taciturn janitors
vs. motionless poetry of sociable professors
vs. poetry spoken to an empty playground
vs. poetry learnt by drunk waitresses
vs. poetry that has not been written
vs. poetry that will never be written
i.e. poetry of the hot textual object
vs. poetry evocative yes but *of what*

Actual Evil

naked french girls smoking weed
naked ecuadorian girls drinking cherryade
naked dutch girls watching philip seymour hoffman dvd
no naked french girls smoking weed

THIRTY-THREE SUNGLASSES

When it Came

I could see clouds in my coffee
clouds in my phone
satellites like the skeletons of dragonflies
were orbiting the planet
from the train I saw a cloud of birds
wow there were birds in my coffee
birds in my phone
as if everything on earth were texting
furiously everything else I could feel
their texts arriving in my body
this has been a blue / green message
exiting the social world

I'm a Buddhist This is Enlightenment

I hate when life like an autobahn explains itself
also when the news presenters share a little joke
alluding to the private world of showbiz bullshit
so Giles had to say 'I can't relate to this' I liked
when Aki whispered something in the pool hall
that remains unknown to most of the universe
and then 'what I just said I'll never say again'
O I'm trying very hard to remember a word
with 'I' and 'O' in it a good amount of mystery
for a Saturday like meeting a really cute couple
or when words touch each other in strange places
like drinking & biography or sex & cheesecake
if I test each object on my desk with heat
under my hand with heat the right one will reply

Heavily

Today is a day of zero connectivity
I brush my teeth and dunk my face in water
which is what you wash your breasts with
I want to use the exact same soap
and drink orange juice probably from Spain
now there is a gelid light in the kitchen
& outside the same air we all have
to breathe the day is in some kind of tank
all I will do is think of increasingly
horrible things to tell you striking the side
of my head for a new image there is no
competing with the spectacular & obvious
am I not a child at the opera of emotions

The Prince

let a man sit down I'm in telesales me
would you buy off this voice on a phone
what do they call you Sarah Sarah Sarah
do you find me attractive Sarah
I don't mind if you don't I'm a bit tipsy
I'm celebrating maybe I'll tell you
if we get to know each other better
Sarah you're beautiful you know
never let a man tell you otherwise
right don't be that way nice girls Sarah
who's your friend Melanie where you from
how old are you woo is it true when
I get you home are you going to let me
spank it I'm going to spank it I'm
going to hold that caramel cheek in
my palm I'm coming round soon later
I love you baby you think I can't hear all
that soft boy shit let her know what
you're going to do she don't want you
she wants me she don't want you she
wants me you may as well delete my
number you had your chance today and
blew it it's Geoffrey Geoffrey with a J

Nobody's Deep

I am very interested indeed
in excessive modes of femininity
without obvious flaws you are impossible
to approach because there is no subject
is it me or do you look slightly russian
no subject apart from your beauty
which is no subject to speak of
would it be best to pledge
love without ever having seen your
face thus making my interest genuine
as it is I am pulled across the ice-rink
by my eyes dizzied in fake rages
when you turn away your face
jealous of your waiter
and as your writer even lowlier
I've never even heard your voice order
a sparkling water and if I did it's true
I might stop caring I'm happiest
with a quarter moon
of cheek a stalker of train
carriages and leaver of lonely notes
I stay two tables away to trade in hope
inventing the reflection's reflection
interested in ice and soap

Guide to the Liberal Cities

tour the museums and charity shops
careful not to purchase anything
in case someone interprets it as art
do not read at the pub speak
of entities in need of authentic substance
be it souls gold or blood
try not to *do* anything
especially like linger
in the butterfly enclosure for a kiss
stay instead inside the reptile house
stinking of skunk
safe in the dry warm dark
don't compare origins with anyone
but remember thinking
'peeling your jeans off each leg
is like skinning a leek'
ignore the prospective tenants
filing through your sleep
by all means make an intrigue of your partner
but remember the bedroom is a gallery
and you should draft an exit
don't remain attached to any project
but defer indefinitely the work
towards your own capture
do not stain the toilet bowl
but taste your breath
and skulk across the early park

Imagine One Lacks a Basic Component

the glimmer or grain inside an actual
person remember those blurry tears
they felt at the time like evidence
planted a sort of elaborate deception
to convince oneself later like a full day
in youth spent practising one's signature
for the writing presumably of cheques

What Do You Think About That

this will probably sound cheesy and weird
but maybe we're a couple of cartoons
let's convince the animators
we're two kinds of animal
let them show our fear and longing
flipping like dark fillets in our bodies
i hope they draw us genitals
a band of dogs with saxophones
or turn us into sexy furniture
dial up our eyes with hearts and dollar signs
every time forever happens

Primal Memory

It isn't you I wish to speak to
but the one who stands directly
behind
who returns to see your room
in the mirror's cruellest angle
water
ties cold rings to his wrists
it tastes like a smooth stone
imagine
someone in the world exists
who wishes harm upon you
tonight
walk with bare feet through the house
and watch light step out of the fridge

AMERICAN HARDCORE

Regular Black

Who wouldn't rather be watching
a film about werewolves instead
of composing friends' funeral playlists
all day I've been suspecting something
like must the 1st thought always
be 'slipping out of her brassiere'
or 'slipping out of her brassiere'
that nobody calls anyone a LIAR anymore
and who misses that unambiguousness
that the word 'image' has for a long time
been inadequate that back then nobody
went invisible among their references
that the silence of the looking glass was total
that pizzas were delivered through the evening
that nobody's left eye wept continuously
that one's ambitions were solely amorous
also tonight would have been perfect weather
to take your girlfriend out for ice-cream
needless to say she remembers it
differently the 2nd thought is
is it possible she's doing it on purpose
and love back then love was a papercut

Welcome to Frick's

I sure hope there isn't someone walking around
with the name 'Frick' that would be a damn shame
the second you open the door you're punched
in the face with the fumes from a million cigarettes
you can't stand in the doorway more than 3 seconds
without smelling like you smoke 10 packs a day
never mind that let's travel inside the bar
lovely plaid carpet adorns this place I didn't know
pool players were so into plaid it all melds perfectly
with the wood panelling cut down a few trees
shoot a few deer come on in to Frick's to unwind
the pool tables have seen better days the pool sticks
all suck and are wobbly and well their stuff just
sucks here that doesn't matter I don't really play pool
all that much anyway let's go get a drink
be prepared to wait at the bar even if they aren't
that busy I don't know why those are just the facts
of life best thing about Frick's has got to be their
prices so what are you waiting for come hang out
with mid-Michigan's finest high-school dropouts
at Frick's the ultimate in service quality convenience
and status can be had right here in Midland MI

The Council of Girls

Today I stand before you
uncertain of my guilt
of what I am accused
or should say sorry for
your eyes are screwed
like knots in wood
filled with the suggestive quiet
of trees gossiping telepathically
maybe it would help
if I recited in an irish accent
or sang a little song
your faces grow more beautiful
as I am wired to the lie detector
crueller yet more pitying
I see there are hundreds of texts
to be read out and correlated
and I am happy to help as best I can
clear up this confusion
clarify and analyse the things I said
while drunk I speak to you
without the hope of mercy
you are everything to me
daughters
I kneel on the ground from which
you sprung
my jury of sunflowers

101/1

If I'm feeling depressed about the inconstancy
of meaning in the world I like to pause this
on your face your face made up of little
blocks of light & try to guess how
deliberate your expression is in
that precise instant how deep
does acting go I can't tell what's
happening at the back of your mind as
you laugh or look surprised does that make
you good at it an art critic thinks that meaning
actually exists somewhere inside the work I unpause
the clip & feelings play across your face each slowing
for the moment they come closest to the surface
the way actors turn away languidly wanting
the lights to touch their cheeks forever
it reminds me of looking up to see
that a train has pulled alongside
mine I'm swapping eyes
with the eyes I met

Best Thing You Can Do Now is Do Nothing

I shouldn't be so mean
that woman in paris wanted money for sugar
a diabetic relieved to find someone english
yes I refused her
I doubt she actually collapsed
or the spanish family on the tube jaundiced
in awful london light going the wrong way
round the circle line
I could have said something
I was playing my game with the little piece
of dirt on the window
moving my head to make it vault
the obstacles at stations
this amoebic sprite
was starting to develop some character
when it cleared the signs at tower hill then monument
the reflection I met in the tunnel
was tinted blue in its commuter's grimace
but inside inside it was rejoicing

Rich / Poor Gap Widens

NA	YA
shadows	coffee
the sea	the light
the moon	eyes
nature generally	value judgement
anglepoises	connectivity
'blue / or was it grey' etc.	paris
domesticity	the 1st person
dramatis personae	romans
mirrors	facts
the 3rd person	jokes
depth	mirrors
greek mythology	sincerity
london	doom

POV

All day I have been watching women
crush ripe tomatoes in their cleavage
whatever you can think of
someone's already done it
there's a new kind of content
pre-empting individual perversions
I've seen my missing girlfriend's face
emerge cresting from a wave of pixels
I sleep with a [rec] light at the foot
of my bed all the film crews
have been infiltrated by
militant anti-pornographers
sometimes in surfaces there is a dark
ellipse it's the cameraman's reflection

All The Happiness You'll Ever Need

the sun in paris rides a skateboard
giving everyone high-fives winking
at a man whose wife leans out from
a first-floor hotel balcony standing
by a fish stall in the still shady streets
of the disgusting latin quarter at 7 a.m.
having violet eyes like you-know-who
and lighting the unlit cigarettes of two
american boys with very serious hair
wearing plain white T-shirts and then
it's off going waterskiing up the seine

Take It Away

The arts must be forced underground
art supported by the state will never
have the balls to honestly question
the situation that produced it
[CHEERS]
Art must be stripped and chased
out of town only the true artist
will survive let the rest open
strip clubs sell meow meow
[CHEERS]
Art will never refuse good money
that would be way too obvious
art always accepts a prize &
spends it on drink & then
passes off some piece
of total crap as art
[CHEERS]
Thus art challenges our situation
in a new & genuine way now
please welcome to the stage
platinum act The Killers
to play a new number
take it away guys
[CHEERS]

ICE-CREAM WEATHER

No Dreams

meet jack and my brother in rough trade
having sat there half an hour already reading
most of muldoon's maggot
these guys are always late
put maggot back on display rack
go to stupid cafe
with dribbly candles & deliberately wobbly tables
staffed by what seems to be jack sparrow
leave go to pellicci's instead
eat pay
walk to the gun near spitalfields
the rugby's on I don't care
jack pretends to care or perhaps does care
drink halfpint of heineken
the world's so responsive right now
texts already from alex sophie tim alex again zeljka steve
meet sophie on her break
oxford street's rammed crazy russians everywhere
money everywhere christmas lights
she orders a baked potato with baked beans
I don't order anything pellicci's wasn't that long ago
when it comes she says she wishes she'd asked for cheese
I take it back and get them to put cheese on it
they don't charge extra
I feel good about that
go to the icelandic reading
feel tired
go round to sophie's when she's done working
she does a good impression of someone
who doesn't want to go to sleep

go to sleep
have sex
no dreams

The Craft

blu-tac hair spit nail-clippings a SIM card
containing the subject's number traces
of the subject physical or associative
it's really very simple the object
will be horrifying in its aspect
to capture something of the violent
nature of attachment having a face eyes
mouth hands feet you must shift your gaze
inversely on the axis of attraction for
why else are you interested & as
the object is 'moved' so the
subject is tenfold 'moved'
so you are 'moved'
a hundredfold

I Was Going to Say

something like 'I take it all back'
and it's not even my line but when
I got to the bar I realised I couldn't feel
my face slipped on a step & got distracted
by 3 girls' smiles & the image of their crotches
buzzing away below the table like 3 cuddly bees

Too Poetic

* {Poetry}, or a relation thereof.
* {Anthony_Ian_Berkeley}, a deceased rapper and hip-hop producer, or a relation thereof.

Fall in Love All Over Again

much against everyone's advice
I have decided to live the life
I want to read about and write it
not by visiting the graves of authors
or moving to london to hear
in my sleep its gothic lullaby
not by going for coastal walks
or being from the north and lathing
every line as an approach it's
way outmoded I run a bath turn
off the lights I think only of
lathering the pale arms of my wife
for now a girl who dreads weekends
then I guess I might as well teach
squandering so as not to squander
this marvellous opportunity right?

Coming Soon

I've watched it 50 60 times my face is inches from the screen
your eyes seem to search my eyes you seem to be reading
these lines you seem to be liking them you look away
you look back it reminds me of watching someone
cleaning a window or a 2-way mirror waiting
for your look to shift to see past the dust
and your own face that would
be what kind of surprise

The White Door

Is that what's happened I honestly feel
like I've been asked to do this by someone
so beneficent I can't possibly refuse
she doesn't speak but her simple look
tells me something is resting on this task
O svelte princess of future states

One Note Solo

it depends if he is genuine or not
if he is it is wonderfully expressive
sensitive overt yet subtle brave art
if he is not it is an arrogance and
conceit a concept daring to see
how stupid people can be how much
they can be conned by confidence
it's a confidence trick that if he gets
pleasure from makes him in my eyes
an arsehole to do something like that
although it could be argued if the
audience are aware of his exhibitionism
and enjoy the twist to a normal stage
performance it is of no matter what his
psychology is and he would not be an
arsehole or a twat only he himself
knows how much of his planned act
however planned is motivated by
honesty and how much is disingenuous
absurdism if that distinction can be made

Personal Statement

hi i should like to have the answers
to shall we say certain questions
and to wake up certain of directions
and a levelness of breathing and
of not being in a neo-noir movie
instead the mildness of the evening
and the possibility of ice-cream
waiting ahead in girlfriend heaven
when i return with gifts one chocolate
one strawberry i'll think of a question
any question the way you might prop
a stick below a window letting in
night air then pick that stick up from
its slant using it to gesture wisely
while elaborating on whatever
making all the time shall we say finer
distinctions splitting pairs of pairs
together like couples who both see
suddenly that this won't be for ever
it takes till now for the window to fall
and there can be no bitterness
or anger so what i'm saying is thank
you thank you and see you later

INFINITY POOL

Buffering 15%

you aren't thinking clearly as you enter the bank
on the day leslie nielson dies
the coldest december 'in living memory'
mark's badge reads
'have a good time all the time'
maybe you should think about getting a motto
maybe you should think about painting the fridge blue again
maybe then you'd feel less like the shape of a person
suggested by the fall of light on a bookcase
you find you're thinking a lot about your friend the monk
who won't share with you his secret
to be sure he is a very complex gentleman
but hardly deep even if he can <u>burn leaves</u>
<u>with nothing but the power of his mind</u>
he is a remorseless self-publicist
maybe that's his secret
or his secret is he doesn't have one
he claims to remember where he buried
a live beetle in a matchbox
but afflicted as you are with awful memories
you're not sure you believe him
filling out the paying-in slip is difficult
maybe you should stop growing your fingernails
'shhh' he went this morning
 pretending to be listening

Chocolate Milk

The sort of really attractive junky sitting
on the wall by the Magdalen Street
drop-in centre who said I looked
4-dimensional and asked me
to dance in the gorgeous
level light of 5.45

Poem in the Dark

okay what if I tell you
I am writing this in 1989
opposite the Taj Mahal
as large ferns shade my diary
with their wingprints and actors
screaming 'this isn't a movie'
are defenestrated you can't trust it
knowing something of the world
it's like the lights are out
and you must listen to my voice
tasting the grey coffee in it
my real name is not decided
and signs me as your co-star
okay stay still a minute
let's see what's really *here*
looking almost invisible
between the windows
not forgiven by your focus
nor giving away a face
to anything that's real or fake
but in this long 'room' somewhere
like a roofless carriage on a train
you can see the trees and lanterns
at the stations speeding overhead
in this long room blown with sun
our feelings are waiting for each other
okay I've stepped into the next one
to say goodbye and even if
you've seen it before to describe
to you its sources of light

It Never Got Any Better

unlike the poems onto which you could plot
a graph of improvement each one a little
more than the last & still there's room
to get even better to keep inching
away from those atavistic
mutants that spawned
a whole species
you took clippings
from their handsomest
sons same way they bred
bananas from genetic fuck-ups
& were able to present ever better
bananas have you noticed they never
have those black seeds in anymore the last
banana is glowing in the centre of your perfect
poem & the problem with it isn't the one of
preserving your origins in dusty drawers
but that it'll be impossible to conceal
all those times you didn't survive
every wrong turn you took
to stamp out your steps

Clones

But for once, I was in control.
Patty is my name titillating how r u.
She's a spooge gutterslut that gives
a good porn fantasy. If you are prepared
and can stand the pain be sure to join
portuguese abuse (actual stills from the movie.
Provocative salsa missies is the most
talked-about reality latina site on the net.
Looking at her in games is definitely a must.
The finest brown-skinned spunks in the world
can be found getting slammed on this porno site.
Lawd do you watch the moon on that hoe.

Is Death Not the End

this is what you couldn't shake
in the basement's earthy dark
your long hair hangs
like a death rocker's your
dirty sneakers swing & even
if it isn't true in the strong light
outside I picture a tree
the quiet held in its branches
its shape shot through hundreds
of windows of which you
dropped between dry rafters
still smelling of summer
are nothing but a root

It's Great to Be Here

and something else happens
a few people who come across my work think
I am in fact a girl I know I really
don't know how it happened well
I started to think what if this idea
was widespread & I did as it happens
think of entering the mslexia comp 1 year
how would I account for this my
presence / appearance at readings
awards ceremonies etc
would I pretend I had a wife
that we shared both names it's possible right
I'd read a speech prepared by her
tonight it would go something
like 'I'd almost given up then I thought
how crushed I'd be
if anyone gave up all those beautiful poems
written off so I stopped pretending
to write poems it's like
everyone simultaneously stops
pretending they are deep or anything
& for that I must excruciate
and thank this guy I take you
as my wholly open-ended subject to have
and to hold there is no separation
you can't be unselfconscious
about doing anything so generous
till death do us part you'll accept
on my behalf the prize'

Miserable I Hope You Do Too

a face becomes more beautiful
as it says it doesn't want to be with you
the cemetery has trees like the memory of fires
this isn't really *like* anything actually sorry
there's the rest of the year to think about it
to become trees or fires or whatever they are
we documented the whole thing remember
that's what we were doing or didn't you notice
I don't want to know which of us wrote it
it's like asking who engraved the gravestones
you're literary why don't you *read* them
guess I can't believe anyone'd want to keep
every note & I thought I would be glad
you called but I'm kind of not

It's All Currency

a student talking showing off about a poem he wrote
for his poetry module about a man who covers
things in post-it notes which apparently his
tutor found 'refreshing' reminds me of
when the artist simon ——— had
taken acid & used post-it notes
to label all the objects in the kitchen
he ran into difficulties when he came to
actual post-it notes each sheet in the morning
covered with very neat microscopic script expanding
many possible uses of these semi-adhesive labels
interesting I just found out post-it notes have
never had an advertising slogan but are
encompassed it would seem finally
by their brand its pertinence
has if anything increased I wonder
now how close the student's poem was
and if he'll have any other ideas

BEAUTIFUL SUNSETS

Way Too Cold

anyway girls look prettier in winter
with ear muffs on bicycles in coats
did she know she'd have that effect
'accidentally' hitting videocall somehow
so when I answered I was looking up
into her face from inside her handbag
pretty weird seeing her suddenly
in a scarf snowflakes whizzing past
streetlights glaring from her shoulder

Dédicace

however bad stricken deceitful it gets
you forgo falseness sleep on leatherette
& there are still goldfronts in the world
mascara stained T-shirts lie detector tests
a 'comfort for the depressed' leaflet
is handed out by some guy in a suit
extreme feelings of needing to be sick &
not breathing can make everything clearer
don't go your friends are having a party
Comfort for the Depressed are playing
I love the beautiful way you don't know
how your sentences will end but arrive
at 'magenta' with genuine surprise
goodnight my friend at least we tried
dead? mon dieu we are *kentucky fried*

Finally Rich

I got a job
I got a job writing poems
oh hi I never met you before
going to write you a poem
about your anniversary
your niece's christening
your son's wedding
your uncle's funeral
you provided a helpful 'factsheet'
full of personal details
your favourite songs and anecdotes
this is my material
the tone is 'light'
the approach is up to me
you will pay £3 a line
you will pay £5 a line
you will pay £7 a line if rhymed
but hang on
wouldn't a real poet want to get at 'truth'
you paid for a real poet
how can I get 'truth' from this 'factsheet'
the only way to 'truth'
is saying 'yo, I don't know you'
and refusing to write the poem in the poem
then I doubt you'd pay me
here's my question
do you want to buy a poem
because you know about poetry
or because you don't know about poetry
think I need to see you

think I need to meet you
think I need to come and stay with you for like a week
perhaps the whole thing will get out of hand
if I get involved in some 'heavy shit'
I'll write a screenplay about it
of course I'll change your name
the names of my dystopian employers
~~charlie kaufman~~ some bigshot director
will buy the script executive produce
and I'll be rich I won't write any more poems
about your uncle's wedding
your son's christening
your niece's funeral
your bill: £210
happy anniversary

My Real Name is Exploded View

it's far too obvious
but then again isn't it
the point isn't that why
they want it like wanting
to know the name of each
part of a car to view the act
from every angle to use every
possible combination of objects
think what I find most astonishing
is watching their expressions gazing
at the darkness of an orifice something
of them is drawn into that desolate socket
a sort of ecstasy ends every stare inside me
& I feel them all like soft explosions in my body

The Blue Balcony

when I went to New Zealand
everyone had a friend who died
now everyone here does too
when Iain last saw me
he said 'how are you Sam
you poor bastard' well quite

You're Sweet

is my sense of self too easily shaken
is my sense of self too dependent
on the things I see and hear
is there such a thing as
being too flexible
am I just easily swayed
too bad if you don't feel this
way if your persona seems 'fixed'
perhaps you should pay some more
attention to what's going on around you
ever listen to contemporary stuff occasionally
instead of the same old records mm maybe
I'd be screwed if I woke up one day
without all my cultural supports
& apparatus hey lucky for me
that will never happen

My Face Saw Her Magazine

across the moonscapes of skateparks you are 13 yrs old
& no longer allowed to play with boys / on platform 6
wearing your amazing cape you are not in fact you
but someone else / while I'm a guy who mishears lyrics
resulting in a more beautiful but private understanding
with your dark fringe white shirt & straw hat you are
the palest goth at the picnic / resolutely uncharmed
by my very charming friend you are the poster of disinterest
in bed & matching underwear you are disguising the tunnel
we dug in the american prison / not answering my texts
what you are is the briefcase glowing with golden contents
I realise I can only look in one eye at a time / it is pure
propaganda the pupil a blot of blackest inkjet ink
in your luxury woollen garment you are an advertisement
for luxury woollen garments / & then & then you wink

Alternative Title Matrix

KILOMETRE ZERO   SPIRIT

PRINTS   BLACK   CARPET   VIDEO

NASTY   MY   ITALICS

JANET   JACKSON   FAKE   LAKES

NO   DREAMS   GREEN

INK   REAL   CREEPS   CRUMB

CREDIT   REPTILE   HOUSE

BEST   TEXTS   HOTEL   BIBLE

SWAN   ATTACK   WHITE

ALBUM   DOUBLE   ZERO   PERFECT

GIBSON   SWEET   MERCH

ALMOST   DEAD   AMERICAN   HARDCORE

CRYSTAL   TITS   GROW

SYSTEMS   SPOOKY   DUST   LAST

LINE   BAD   ORANGE

ROBERT   LOWELL   SWITCHES   PENCILS

Time Please

I have heard your poetry
Mr Cruise and I do not
think it is very good
you stand behind the bar
in the blue light they use
to stop heroin addicts
locating a vein but
it will not stop you locating
your 'vein' as it were loudly
and in public in my country
you do not need to shout
a poem that is pretty much
the definition of a poem
Mr Cruise I don't drink
alcohol so I can't relate
to your performance and
in my opinion you should
be punished for your
outburst not rewarded

THE NEW SINCERITY

Nobody Famous

This is me eating not 1 not 2 but 3 pancakes
this is me having Breakfast in America in paris
with my creepy associates
this is me punching a photographer
this is me listening to my ansaphone messages
these are my new converse all****s
this is me logging into my email
I think my password 40 times a day
what kind of effect is that having
here I am inside the reptile house
this is me examining the roofs on my street
to see on which the snow has melted meaning
the neighbours are growing hydroponic skunk
this is me playing dolphin olympics
this is me reading akhmatova while listening
to arthur russell and the feeling is mutual
this is me planning my comeback
cutting my hair at 20 to 4 in the morning
here I am in a wet field as a clown tells me to 'get real'
here are my eyes suddenly in the train window
this is me surrounded by the sounds of cheap suits
these are my reviews they may contain spoilers
this is me smoking a moth for 10 dollars
this is me having my extremely nuanced feelings
overwhelmed by pop music and kind of enjoying it
this is me trying to remember a word
this is me watching a clip of a hipster being struck
in the head by a pigeon and laughing too loudly
this is me in the grip of my jealousies
this is me pointing at a rainbow

here I am running back and forth along the train
showing the rainbow to my fellow passengers
this is me glancing down at my outfit
every 5 minutes it seems I can't help it
here I am listening to the 7th symphony
this is me in public putting on a 2nd pair of sunglasses
because I feel suddenly like crying
here I am defining my personal space.

Forgeries

yes so it would appear it is time to as it were
come clean I found these poems sheaved
inside a photocopier at my university
two polish girls were reproducing
free beer vouchers the sheets
were folding from the slot
still hot someone made
about 1000 copies
of them from
here on the tone
may delicately shift
this is a disclaimer & a
warning with the manuscript
rolled up in my back pocket I feel
like a collaborator in my fate an evil twin
mixing in the canteen with dunces & hot asians

Thumbnails

torture is when the mind
is inseparable from the body
it is the making a point of this
the heads of the massive sunflowers
weigh almost as much as human heads
I was lying in a bathtub filled with petals
and later someone touched me on the subway
perhaps the real horror is that we are used
to being able to escape I look oriental
but my grandfather was german
and I have the pinkest nipples
riding past the empty greenhouses
I was thinking of undoing my blouse
and when my blouse rode up it opened
little diamonds between the buttons and there
was my skin I imagined the greenhouses
in flames then everything was made
of little diamonds it was a unit
that felt completely natural

Good Morning Stupid

there's nothing out there now
but some pretty annoying clouds
a landscape used to advertise butter
phones keep ringing in the other houses
hello sounds   of the new mills
all the call centres of lincolnshire & lancashire

Special New Brand

what am I doing here
thought I liked you
guys thought we
shared something
similar suspicions
about culture now
everyone is singing
your songs I used to
listen to this one / on
my minidisc player
trying to get some
sleep in lousy
australia now I'm
feeling like a fucking
alien feeling betrayed
I have to accept you
sold out just like the
others I / m the same
as all these assholes
this 37 yr-old balding
website designer in a
flatcap headbanging
to the haircut song
dudes srsly starting to
think I'd rather go 2
church

The Clot

I wish for the destruction of the rainforests
to continue or what would be the point
in recycling just as I wish for your
renunciation fetish to be upheld
or where is the reward in wanting
I wish my glasses were tinted 1 degree
towards dusk & noon was a touch brighter
I felt more keenly the pain of no longer
being a marxist that I didn't have
to follow girls in the galleries
of modern art but met
someone with no vaccination
scar on her bicep or I was sipping
on elemental vodka with glacial ice
or was nuzzling the sweetest intersection
of a 7-foot woman I relish a precise
anxiety when writing my wishes
I have not undertaken this
lightly and cannot
discount the
results I'm glad if
I scare easily this matches
not my desire to blaspheme with
'a new sincerity' it's not called that I
want to see clearly each thing taken from me

Hey Perverts

if I know you and I thiiink I do
I think I know the kinds of things
you like like putting the heating
up full & walking round in your shorts
with the windows open like buying
organic mince & flushing it straight
down the toilet as soon as you get in
like searching for stunt deaths & funfair
accidents like deliberately changing
your mind like walking a metre behind
someone on their way home at night
like photographing every item of
clothing you own like sitting in pubs
alone putting out creepy vibes like
saying 'bad dog' to a good dog like
making up stuff for your counselling
session & different stuff for your parents
like wasting x2 an unethical lunch
like saying you haven't seen the movie
when you have & studying my reactions
as we watch it like me telling you this
stuff especially that like busying yourself
with your web of lies if this isn't enough
which it obviously isn't then I have
something here extremely interesting
isn't it yesterday's horoscope which we
can test rigorously for accuracy here's
where each thing finds its hollow place

Help Yourself

Are you concerned about the use of special effects
Have you visited at night the observatory on its tall hill
Do you believe they've starting cloning humans
Have you imagined what it's like to actually squeeze a swan's neck
This is necessary if we are to continue assisting your recovery
Does imagining a god make you feel more playful
Does your face appear increasingly like the reflection of a battered
heart
Are you enjoying the chillout soundtrack to this cassette
Ever mistaken your hand for someone else's
Have you not informed the relevant authorities
With your headphones on can you walk forever
Does it make you feel kind of powerless
Have you not received permission from the companies you
mentioned
Did you bless the gap with meaning
Did you derive any pleasure from it
Do you hear at night the slow creep of history
Are you feeling depressed
Do you harbour a dread of the obvious
Was there evidence of a struggle
Does it seem that no one dies anymore yet they do disappear
Have you ever simultaneously googled a drop of water
Do you regret not getting married
What do you remember
Do you know what happens if you fail to complete the
questionnaire
Did you hear about the woman in minnesota who failed to
complete the questionnaire
Would you say you are a generous person

Of what are you more afraid dying or suffering

How did you come to be here in our care

Is this in any way helping

Are the wires coming out of your head attached to a lie detector

or an mp3 player

Do you have a brain up your sleeve

Is it still too soon

See how fast you can forward this one

Personal Ad

opposite me at the table seat
you were looking cute in blue
blue jeans to be fair you weren't
actually that pretty but I borrowed
your *Observer* & suppressed a sneeze
you seemed interested in politics & me
your party had a new leader I began paying
attention only when I noticed you were getting
off at Nottingham altogether things I thought had
gone pretty well we'd even laughed at the same picture
of the loser running a finger along his strong even hairline
I should have written my number in your sudoku who knows
you seemed the sort to read as a matter of principle the entire paper

81 Austerities

1 sets out stall as critique of poetry & arts institutions
2 porn theme overlaying 'heart & mind'
3 continuation of porn theme
4 alienation chiefly from romantic 'cliché'
5 not sure how this works – I imagine it is arbitrary
6 back to porn in two registers
7 the voice so far is coalescing into something. Henceforth poetic bits will be highlighted in yellow
8 the titles remain enigmatic
9 well, yes, this nails something not particularly worth nailing (implies present poet is beyond & above all this)

10 back to leitmotif of porn, last line a parody of some sort. Pretty
11 yes, this is fine, the slightly recondite vocabulary that is cool with something somewhere
12 this is lovely and funny
13 modulating in last two to distinct dramatis personae
14 enigmatic title (taken from *Resident Evil*?) Good
15 another alienation device complete with joke
16 not sure what's going on here: the contexts elude me, I have no grasp on them
17 nicely sinister, though I wonder about its relationship to the porn theme
18 yeees, sort of, ok, worth keeping

19 indeed of 'what'? – not sure this does anything except say, 'I'm different, I'm better'
20 see 19
21 ok, another one rattling on with assurance
22 re: the book? scepticism gets a bit stifling at times
23 that old alienation, the paper will not cut the poem
24 I wonder about the valency of lines like the last one
25 yep
26 yep
27 back to porn (ok subtext devalued objectified desire)

28 yep

29 ok . . . a touch of surrealism in the night, but a poem that needs to be accompanied by other poems

30 the disjunction of these two lines is emblematic of the psychological mechanism of much of the work

31 the old irony that cannot take any emotion quite seriously . . . as if there were nothing but inverted commas and porn

32 ok

33 ok ok

34 see 31. We know there is no accident, you were not dying, we know that this is literary proposition

35 ok

36 quite, see 31 etc.

37 almost perfect title for complete set (or for a band)

38 perfectly justified and all, perhaps more worth saying

39 another dramatis personae, well carried off

40 once again, seems to underpin the whole collection

41 what business?

42 yes, fine, the overheard dramatis personae

43 Hiroshima signifies what?

44 ok ok

45 ok – as well to know, but then that's the point, a found poem grinning at itself

46 ok

47 and what makes it pretentious (not that it isn't)?

48 not sure, seems very slight, but then maybe slight's the point. I still don't care for it

49 more postmodernism?

50 you mean cemetery not cemetery?

51 a little tedious? Keep the end?

52 enough?

53 ok

54 the thing is you have covered this kind of territory in other poems

55 ok

56 back on the institutional arts thing. Peter Reading was doing similar things in the late 70s/early 80s

57 Yes, now this is good, there is a genuine curiosity and experienced bleakness

58 back on the ironic high horse?

59 funny, ok, but have we had enough about poetry? I mean it will amuse other students of poetry but, to adopt a voice I didn't know I possessed, I doubt it means jackshit out there

60 heavy pastiche in green?

61 good

62 yes, the broken compulsive narrative is not just about narrative, i.e. itself

63 neat, yes

64 ok, funny

65 ok, better than the band names for my money

66 ok

67 I have nothing against the old sincerity of course, but then I have lived with it a good while

68 the poem seems to reach towards the tragic, in that it has to accept both irony and tears. They generally have a hard time together. That is the tragedy. But it's well to be reminded of the world beyond inverted commas, even if it's tragic

69 reminds us of its postmod provenance again. Do we need reminding?

70 yes, this voice holds

71 yes, the echo of Edward Thomas at the end ...

72 there's luck and luck

73 so-so

74 better!

75 a bit *too* up itself?

76 the long long poem is obscure and 'wived' seems a bit wrong – at least it calls a lot of attention to itself. Very nice end though

77 ok, maybe over reflective? (even in the up-itself mode, that is)

78 hmmmm

79 funny

80 hm, ok, but not that much – more up-the-poetry lark stuff

81 not sure if obedience is the word

Index